EXPLORING THE
SIXTH SENSE

EXPLORING THE SIXTH SENSE

An Introduction to Performance Mentalism

DR. JAMES E. JONES

Outskirts Press, Inc.
Denver, Colorado

Outskirts Press, Inc.
http://www.outskirtspress.com

ISBN: 978-1-4327-4450-2

Outskirts Press and the "OP" logo are trademarks belonging to Outskirts Press, Inc.

CONTENTS

DEDICATION

To my wife and children: I wish you much
love and gratitude for your infinite patience.

ACKNOWLEDGEMENTS

I would like to thank those creative and innovative individuals who have dedicated their professional careers to the study, development and performance of mentalism. I am always impressed by the level of professionalism demonstrated by those who have chosen to devote their considerable talents to this field of entertainment.

INTRODUCTION

I remember performing my first mentalism routine. I was twelve years old at the time. One Saturday, my brother asked my mother if he could bring his new girlfriend to dinner the next Sunday. During his small talk about the girl and her family, he mentioned that her 11-year-old pet dog, **Dee Dee**, had passed away a week earlier and that her entire family was really taking it hard. I was sitting in the family room and neither my mother nor brother knew I had overheard the conversation. Mom said it was okay and that she would have lunch ready about noon.

The next Sunday I was obligated to perform, as I did for almost all of our guests, my 30-minute magic show. This included a vanishing clock, egg bag, sucker sliding die box, comedy milk pitcher followed by the final effect, the Zombie. As always, as an encore, I was ready with the "pick–a–card" trick accomplished by a simple card force (the only one I still use today!). For the card effect, I always "forced" the Eight of Hearts. While cleaning up from the show and waiting for my mother to "suggest" if I could do "just one more trick" for our guest, I would go to the bathroom and get ready to force the Eight of Hearts. Returning to the living room, I would complete the force and have the volunteer write the name of the card on a small piece of paper. I would then hold the deck in my hand and "divine" the name of the card. It always got a decent reaction.

Recently, I had been told by several "older members" at a Magic Club Meeting (fourteen-year-olds) that instead of doing a card trick, I should try a "mentalism" routine as my encore effect. If I could "obtain" some personal information about an individual at the show that they did not know I had, I could ask them (in general terms about the information, etc.) and then reveal the information in some "mysterious" way. This seemed like a good time to try something new in that no one knew I had any information about the recent death of the family's dog.

After cleaning up from my show, I went to the bathroom and moistened my right index finger with water, then rubbed it briskly on a bar of soap. I then wrote a large **D. D.** on my left wrist (pulse area) in soap, thoroughly dried the writing, and returned to the living room just in time for my mother to suggest an "encore" trick. I asked the young woman if she would like to help me. She said I was "cute" and agreed. I brought out the small piece of paper and began telling her that I did sense that she had gone through a difficult time in the past several weeks. To my surprise, she immediately said that she and her family had suffered a "loss". I told her not to tell me what it was, but to think of the cause of the trauma. By this time, my mother and brother were staring intently at me. I had never done this before and they had no idea that I had any information about the dog! I took the paper and scribbled on it, folded it and placed it in the ashtray. I then took a match, lit the paper and let it burn thoroughly until only ashes were left. I asked the girl to concentrate on the cause of her loss. I then dipped my index finger in the ashes and rubbed the ashes on my arm where I had written the letters in soap. There, in large letters, appeared **D. D.**

What happened next was a source of irritation for my mother for years to come. The girl slumped back in her chair; eyes wide open with tears beginning to well up in both eyes. She looked at me and began to cry. She stood up, excused herself, and went directly to the bathroom. My mother asked me why I had purposely hurt her feelings. I told her that I was completely surprised by the reaction and had no idea that she would react in such a way. Obviously, the pet's death was still a source of anguish and identifying the name was traumatic. I intensely realized there and then the potential impact, and the responsibility, in performing mentalism. This realization has remained with me over the years.

The basis of performance mentalism is the performer's ability to convincingly demonstrate unusual ability with respect to the various aspects of Extrasensory Perception (ESP), often called the "Sixth Sense". Mentalists proficient in using their Sixth Sense abilities apparently receive information beyond the ordinary five senses of hearing, sight, smell, taste and touch. Sixth Sense phenomena are traditionally classified into three main categories. These are: (1) **telepathy**, the awareness of the thoughts or feelings of another person; (2) **clairvoyance**, or awareness of objects, events, or people without the use of the known senses; and (3) **precognition**, or the knowledge of future events.

The main purpose for writing this volume is to provide the reader interested in performance mentalism a **basic** foundation for study and performance. Each effect described in the various chapters can be constructed from common materials at a very reasonable cost. If materials are required commercially from magic dealers, information is provided where they can be located from multiple sources. After reading the routines described in this text, the individual will have an understanding of methodologies and performance criteria to develop a successful mentalism presentation. Additionally, experienced magicians are provided proven routines in which they can adapt for their current presentations if they wish to do so. Information is provided on ways in which to develop and personalize routines that have proven successful in a wide range of audiences and venues.

As with any volume of this type, I have made a good-faith effort to identify individuals who have developed or offered improvements to specific routines. If I have failed to credit any individuals for their work, I assure you it was unintentional.

CHAPTER ONE
Set The Stage!!

One of the most important aspects associated with performance mentalism is that you "set the stage" for your performance. The importance of a brief pre-talk to establish the atmosphere for the performance is significant. It is also important to establish that you are not an "all knowing, all seeing mystic". If you take this conservative approach, you will find that the audience will be more impressed with your abilities and more understanding if you are not always completely successful during your presentation. I find it more believable for the audience if the performer states that, while you are experienced in mentalism, you are certainly not a mystic (unless you are stating to be one).

I feel it is also important to establish at the beginning of your performance that no prior arrangement has made with any member of the audience to help you in a dishonest way. By stating that you may, or may not, be successful in all of tonight's performance, the audience is made aware of the difficulties inherent in mentalism, and sometimes failing is "part and parcel" with the profession. You are not super human, only an individual gifted in some aspects of what is often called the Sixth Sense.

The following is an example of the pre-talk I routinely use prior to beginning my performance. It takes only one to two minutes to complete and "sets the stage" for the performance. This is only an example. Individual performers should develop a similar statement, in their own words, that reflects their individual preferences and presentation situation.

PRE-TALK

I would like to thank you for inviting me here this evening.

Each of us goes through life interacting with the world around us using the five physical senses of hearing, sight, smell, taste and touch. Although these are remarkable abilities, experience has demonstrated that approximately 20% of individuals have the ability to gain additional information from their surroundings using information obtained outside of the five basic senses. Some people call this intuition, premonition, déjà vu or extra sensory perception. No matter what term is used, they are usually classified as aspects of our Sixth Sense. It is our Sixth Sense that is often associated with the more unusual aspects of our existence and may concentrate on events of the past, present and future. It is aspects of our Sixth Sense that we are going to concentrate on this evening.

From the start there are two things I want to briefly mention. First, I make no claim to have all powers associated with the Sixth Sense. I am not psychic and I do not talk to dead people! Over the years I have read hundreds of books and articles pertaining to the Sixth Sense. Everything I am going to attempt tonight comes from over 45 years of study and performance. Many of these effects could be accomplished by almost every individual here if they are willing to devote the time, effort and study to do so.

Second, I have not asked any individual here this evening to help me in any way. Nothing has been pre-arranged. Everything I attempt is going to be spontaneous and, I hope, entertaining.

With that said, let's begin!!

THOUGHTS ON EFFECTS: KEEP IT SIMPLE!!

The following requirements are often considered important in the selection of compelling mentalism effects. These are only suggestions. Others you prefer may be added as you feel appropriate. They include:

1. Whenever possible, you should use straightforward, uncomplicated methods that allow **emphasis on presentation**. If you are required to memorize a list of words, numbers, etc., the use of "back-up cue cards" hidden within the physical materials of the effect (notepad, hand-held blackboard / dry eraser board) should be used to provide the performer a "safety net" should one be necessary.

2. Be sure to use simple, everyday looking props. If your props are brightly colored with elaborate decorations, the audience may identify them as magic props. The effects should be easy to construct using readily available materials.

3. Little or no manipulative skills should be required. Emphasis should be on presentation, not on demanding sleight of hand moves.

4. Effects are easily understood and suited for a wide range of audiences and venues.

5. The length of the effect should be appropriate. A complicated mathematical effect lasting 10 minutes will, most likely, lose interest to the average audience.

6. Use effects that are not "angel dependent" in that an individual seated to the side of the performer might see a secret door, etc., which is used in a prop to complete the effect.

7. A comprehensive, compelling and personalized "patter" story has been developed to be presented with the effect. This is considered essential for a successful presentation.

Table 1 can be used to "score" effects you are considering for your final program. You might find that a given effect scores "Fair or Average" in its present form, but can greatly improved by addressing an area of weakness (example: a comprehensive "patter" has now been developed with an old score of 1 and new score of 4 or 5). You can Xerox the table and score each of your present effects for comparison. Any necessary adjustments to your present routines can be made as each is scored and compared. It is always helpful to seek additional critique(s) from individuals who have observed your performances and you trust for honest opinions (spouse/significant other, close friends, fellow magicians/mentalists in your local magic society, etc.).

Table 1

Item for Consideration	Subjective Rating Scale 1 to 5 1 = poor, 2 = fair, 3 = average, 4 = good and 5 = great				
The use of straightforward, uncomplicated methods that allow **emphasis on presentation.**	1	2	3	4	5
The use of simple, everyday looking props.	1	2	3	4	5
Little or no manipulative skills required.	1	2	3	4	5
Effects are easily understood and suited for a wide range of audiences and venues.	1	2	3	4	5
The length of the effect is appropriate.	1	2	3	4	5
Effect is not "angel dependent".	1	2	3	4	5
A comprehensive, compelling and personalized "patter" story has been developed.	1	2	3	4	5
Total Range (7 to 35)					

*Overall Total Subjective Scale
7 to 15 = **Fair**. The audience has little reaction to the effect.
16 to 29 = **Average**. Good, but not great, audience reaction.
30 to 35 = **Great**. The audience goes crazy when you present the effect!

The importance of using this rating scale is to stimulate the performer to critically evaluate each effect from a variety of viewpoints. An effect using cards may be outstanding, but the performer uses several card flourishes (single-handed deck cut, a card fan to show the faces of the cards, etc.) hinting to the audience that the performer is using sleight of hand, not his mental abilities, to accomplish the effect. A rather simple spreading, almost clumsy, showing of the cards is more appropriate in most instances. This fact alone can improve the overall effectiveness of the effect to one of miracle status! Critically analyze each of your effects (adding any other personal factors you feel appropriate) in an effort to make each as strong and effective as possible.

Selecting Audience Volunteers

Having engaging and responsive audience members help you present interesting effects are essential to your success as a performer. It is important to identify volunteers from the audience that will be a positive addition to your program. Factors to remember in identifying successful volunteers include attractive individuals that are well dressed, have been actively engaged (good eye contact) with you during your "pre-talk" (instead of talking to those around them in a disinterested manner), are not intoxicated or boisterous, and appear interested in your invitation to join you on stage. You should begin to evaluate audience members even before you are introduced. This "screening" process will help you identify potential volunteers without them being aware that you are doing so. Someone who is loud or has "had a few too many" can often appear unaffected if asked to help you on stage. Observing the audience before your program starts can help you prevent making a poor decision in volunteer selection.

For many mentalism effects it is advantageous to have a female volunteer. Their reactions are often more animated and show real emotion in reaction to a given effect. That is not to say that male volunteers are not valuable. You will make the final decision concerning whether female or male volunteers are best for any given routine. Experience will help you to consistently identify volunteers that will enhance your performance. If you need to ask someone to return to their seat because of inappropriate behavior (see heckling section below) please do so in a positive manner.

Audience Heckling

No matter how well the performer has prepared his performance, how entertaining and professional he is in his delivery, there are times when an audience member may interrupt the performance in an inappropriate way. This is especially true if alcohol has being consumed either before or during the performance. Unfortunately, some individuals feel that their inappropriate or disruptive comments are being enjoyed by others in the audience and that attention is being directed to them and away from the performer. The performer must **ALWAYS** remember to never lose their composure no matter the degree of disruption an individual might present. This will happen to the novice and experienced performer at some time during their performance career. The way in which the performer handles the situation can have a dramatic impact on the individual presentation and on their career.

If an audience member begins to make statements that are inappropriate and are interfering with the performer's ability to complete his contract obligations, a very direct and low-key approach should be used to address the problem. The performer may look directly at the offending individual and ask him to again state his concern so the performer may address it in a calm and direct way. Usually this initial interaction will stop the individual. If the individual continues to be disruptive, the performer can ask the audience members if they have the same concerns being expressed by the individual. Peer pressure from other audience members will usually stop the individual from again acting out. In extremely rare instances, if the individual continues to be disruptive, the performer may have to stop the performance and ask for assistance from those in charge of the evening's activities.

Again, it cannot be emphasized enough to **NEVER, NEVER LOSE YOUR TEMPER** and always respond in a professional manner when addressing this unfortunate situation. The audience members enjoy being entertained and realize that the performer cannot continue if he is constantly being interrupted by such an individual.

CHAPTER TWO
Playing Cards and Their Use in Mentalism Routines

Although there has been, and always will be, a great deal of discussion concerning the use of playing cards in mentalism, most performers believe their use is appropriate. One of the most important aspects of using cards is not to give the appearance of being highly skilled in sleight of hand. If the performer appears to be an expert in flourishes and single-handed cuts, the audience will immediately form the impression that what they are about to see is a magic trick and not an experiment in mentalism. For that reason the performer should make every effort possible not to appear proficient in the handling of cards. Additionally, the performer should remember that every person in the audience may not have used regular playing cards to any great extent. The prospective volunteer should be asked if they play card games and know the suits and card values in a deck.

I personally feel it is important that, if possible, the performer use no specially prepared decks, especially in impromptu situations. It is even better if the deck can be borrowed, giving the appearance of no prior preparation. Of course this can not always be accomplished, and you should have a deck of cards readily available when needed. Always ask those assisting you to look at the face and backs of the cards as you display them in a casual manner. There are literally hundreds of outstanding mentalism effects using a deck of playing cards. The following effects may be presented in an impromptu fashion. They are straightforward and require no special sleight of hand.

THE POWER OF TOUCH

In this impromptu routine the mentalist begins by emphasizing the importance of touch in our everyday lives. You can tell the audience that, as an example, when an individual loses one of the five physical senses (hearing, sight, smell, taste and touch), an increase of one of the other senses is often developed to make up for this deficiency. As an example of this phenomenon, you will demonstrate the ability for touch to be developed in a most unusual fashion.

Performance

The mentalist begins by taking a deck of cards from their case and casually showing their faces are all different. Spread the deck from one hand to the other and ask your performer to stop at any point. Have them look at the card and show the card to another individual for verification later in the effect. Now have them place the card anywhere within the deck. Ask your volunteer to shuffle the deck thoroughly, replace the deck in its case, and put the deck on the table.

Ask your volunteer if you may hold their right hand and place your index finger over the pulse of the individual's hand. Ask the individual to close their eyes as you say "red or black". Repeat saying red or black again. Tell the individual that their pulse rate definitely changed as you indicated the color red. Now call out the two red suits "diamonds or hearts". Repeat diamonds or hearts again, and say that their pulse rate again changed when you indicated hearts. Now begin to go through the cards within the heart suit starting with ace, 2, 3, 4, 5, 6, 7, 8, 9, 10, Jack, Queen and King. Repeat this again slowly and indicate their pulse began to speed as you said Queen. Ask the individual if the card they chose was indeed the Queen of Hearts. The individual will identify that the card chosen was, indeed, the Queen of Hearts!! This is a powerful example of the power of touch.

Method

The basis of this effect is the ability of the performer to force a card of choice. It is not the aim of this explanation to discuss the various methods of forcing cards. Many references are available for the individual to identify a method that meets their respective needs. I would suggest a simple method requiring little "flash". Remember the need to appear rather "clumsy" with cards. In this example the Queen of Hearts was chosen to be the force card. If you have a female assistant, this card is of special significance. If you ask women to quickly name a card within the deck, many will respond the Queen of Hearts. Once the Queen of Hearts has been forced, the rest of the presentation is essentially showmanship. Do not rush the process of identifying the card. Make sure to identify the color of the suit first, followed by the suit, and finally identify the specific card. Although this is a relatively simple effect, to a lay audience, it appears to be quite miraculous.

Materials Needed

A regular deck of playing cards

Additional Scenario

If you should happen to drop the deck during the performance, calmly pick the cards up and "peek" at the new card you are going to "force" on the volunteer. The method you elect to force the card is at your discretion.

DUAL VISION

This is a wonderful impromptu effect, using an unprepared deck of cards, which can be presented under the most demanding conditions.

Performance

The mentalist removes a deck of cards from its case the shows that all cards are different. He gives the deck to a volunteer to shuffle, which is then returned to the performer. He turns the cards face up and intently concentrates on the deck as he spreads the cards from hand to hand. He sets the deck face down in front of him and picks up a three-inch square piece of paper. He writes a prediction on the paper, the contents of which is not seen by the volunteer, folds the paper in half and then in half again. The volunteer is asked to cut the deck anywhere they wish and to place the two halves, side by side, on the table. The performer takes the piece of folded paper and places it on top of the cut-off part of the deck. The volunteer is asked to place the lower half of the deck on top, thus completing the cut.

The performer relates that earlier that evening he had a *premonition* concerning several playing cards that might be important during this performance. He asks the volunteer if he has ever had a feeling that something was going to happen before it actually did. Several minutes of similar discussion can also be made with others in the audience concerning their experiences with premonitions in their dally experiences. The volunteer is now asked to gently separate the deck where the card above and below the folded piece of paper is found. The card above and the card below the paper are positioned side by side on the table with the slip of paper between them. The volunteer is now asked to take the folded paper, open it, and reveal what is written on the paper. Written in bold print on the paper is the Two of Hearts and the Five of Spades. When the two cards are turned over by the volunteer, they are indeed the Two of Hearts and the Five of Spades. The performer was indeed correct concerning his earlier premonition.

Method

A deck of cards is removed from its case and handed to a volunteer for inspection to make sure all cards are different. The volunteer is asked to shuffle the deck and hand it back to the performer when they are satisfied that the deck has been thoroughly mixed. The performer casually spreads the face up cards remembering the top and bottom cards of the deck. In this example the top card is the Two of Hearts and the bottom card was the Five of Spades. The performer now false shuffles the deck, giving the appearance of again mixing the cards, while in fact leaving the top and bottom cards in place. The volunteer is now asked to cut the deck and place the two halves side by side on the table. The performer picks up the paper and writes the names of the two cards already mentioned, folds it as described above. The performer places the prediction on the top half of the deck and the volunteer is asked to complete the cut. The prediction sheet is now located between the original top card in the deck (Two of Hearts) and the bottom part of the deck (Five of Spades).

The performer now spends a few minutes discussing premonition as it may pertain to the volunteer's daily experience. The performer can also involve other spectators present in this discussion. The importance of this diversion is to provide a period of time between the "card work" and the prediction being revealed. If completed too soon, an audience member may be able to connect the placement of the prediction and its physical relationship to the top and bottom card of the deck. Once the discussion has come to its conclusion, the performer asks the spectator to gently separate the deck and to identify (but not look at) the card above and below the prediction. The two cards will be placed side by side with the prediction between them. Once the two prediction cards are named, the volunteer is asked to turn each card over and reveal that the performer's premonition was correct.

Materials Needed

A regular deck of playing cards. A blank three-inch square piece of paper.

PRE-FOUR THOUGHT

This is a "packet effect" that will take a few minutes to construct but is well worth the effort. It is always ready and leaves a positive impression on the audience.

Performance

The mentalist states that he will be presenting several effects this evening and would like to identify an individual that is "receptive" to working with him. To do this, he has with him a little "experiment" to present to the audience. A volunteer is identified and the performer produces a brown manila envelope about 3.5 x 6.5 inches, which opens at one end. The performer opens the envelope, with the flap face up, and removes a small packet of four playing cards held together by a paperclip.

Removing the paperclip, the performer places the four cards, in a row right to left, face up in the following order: Queen of Spades, Ten of Diamonds, Nine of Hearts and Three of Clubs. The volunteer is asked to mentally select one of the cards and to visualize the chosen card in his mind. After several moments of "intense concentration", the performer asks the volunteer to identify the chosen card: (Four possible results are described below)

Scenario 1: If the volunteer names the Queen of Spades, the performer states that he had a feeling that was going to be the Queen of Spades. He shakes the envelop identifying that something still remains within. He opens the envelope, flap facing UP, and produces the Queen of Spades.

Scenario 2: If the volunteer names the Ten of Diamonds, the performer states that he had a feeling that it was going to be the Ten of Diamonds at which time he turns the envelope over, and printed on the face of the envelope is: "You will pick the Ten of Diamonds".

Scenario 3: If the volunteer names the Nine of Hearts, the performer states that he had a feeling that it was going to be the Nine of Hearts.

He shakes the envelop identifying that something remains within. He opens the envelope, flap facing DOWN (care taken not to show the writing on the envelope by covering it with the left hand) and produces the Nine of Hearts.

Scenario 4: If the volunteer names the Three of Clubs, the performer states that he had a feeling that it was going to be the Three of Clubs at which time he turns over the three other cards showing that their backs are all BLUE. He then turns over the Three of Clubs showing that it is the only card with a RED back.

Method

This is a "four out" principal in which for any card chosen, the performer is able to demonstrate that he has correctly predicted that card. You will need to do the following to prepare the effect. The four cards used are at the discretion of the performer. I would suggest using four different cards of different suits. In this example, one card should be a low count card (Three of Clubs); one card should be a face card (Queen of Spades); with the two remaining count cards having values between the first two cards (Nine of Hearts and Ten of Diamonds). You will need a duplicate card for the face card and one of the two middle cards (Queen of Spades and Nine of Diamonds in this example). These cards are glued back to back. The low count card (Three of Clubs) will need to have a back color different from the other three. In this example, the Three of Clubs has a red back with the other three cards having blue backs.

The name of the remaining middle card (Ten of Diamonds) is written on the front of the envelope ("You will pick the Ten of Diamonds").

Care should be taken to place the writing around the middle of the front of the envelope and towards the top third. If needed, when you turn the envelope over, your left hand will be able to thoroughly cover the writing and the envelope top will appear blank. To complete the preparation, the double-sided card (Queen of Spades and Nine of Hearts) is placed in the envelop with the Queen of Spades facing the same direction as the open flap (UP) and the Nine of Hearts facing toward the envelop top (flap DOWN). The presence of the double-sided card is not known by the volunteer, with care being taken not to expose the card when the packet of four cards is initially removed. If one of these two cards are chosen, be sure to shake the envelope prior to removing the card. The sound of the card moving within the envelope will be surprising for many. The volunteer, having demonstrated they are "receptive" to your mental abilities, can now be asked to help you with your next effect. This is an effect that can be presented without fear of angles and can be reset in a few moments.

Materials Needed

You will need an opaque 3.5 x 6.5 inch manila envelope. I would suggest you purchase a box of at least 100 of these envelopes in that several effects in this publication use this size envelope.

You will need regular size playing cards identified above. If you decide to construct a stage presentation for this effect, you can use Jumbo size playing cards (Bicycle Jumbo Playing Cards).

Additional Thoughts

The "purest" may be concerned that the two cards glued together may be noticed. As the card is never handled by the volunteer, this should not be a problem. If you are concerned, you can purchase a deck of random double-faced cards (a double-faced deck) from a dealer and find a combination card that meets the requirements of the effect.

If you do not wish to have a card back that is different (three blue and one red back card in this example) you can take a permanent marker and place a large "X" on the back of the indicated card. I feel that the color difference is very effective, but individual preferences always win out!

This effect is certainly applicable for the club environment. The performer can use Jumbo cards for better visibility. An 8" x 10" envelope can be used to secure the Jumbo pack of the four cards along with a Jumbo double-faced card. Upon removing the cards from the larger envelope, the performer can lean each card against its own wine glass. Care should be taken that the angles assure the blue back Jumbo card (or one with an "X" on the back) is not seen by members of the audience during the performance. The remainder of the performance is as described above.

RED, WRITE AND BLUE PREDICTION

Performance

In this effect the mentalist uses two decks of cards, one with blue backs and one with red backs. A volunteer is identified and is asked to pick one of the decks. In this instance, the blue deck is chosen and the performer asks the volunteer to place the deck in their pocket. The performer opens and removes the red deck and casually shows that all the faces are different, and that the backs of the cards are all red. The deck is thoroughly shuffled, placed back in its case and set on the table. The blue deck is now removed from the volunteer's pocket and handed to the performer. The performer opens the card case, removes the cards and shows that all the faces are different, and that the backs of the cards are all blue. The deck is now fanned by the performer and the volunteer is asked to say "stop" at any time. He does so and a card is removed, noted by the volunteer and replaced in the deck. The deck is thoroughly shuffled and replaced in its case. The performer now takes a 3" by 4" sheet of paper from his pocket and requests the volunteer to concentrate on the chosen card. The performer then writes a message on the paper, folds it several times, and places it on the table. The volunteer is asked to identify the chosen card. He identifies the Eight of Hearts. The paper is opened and the following message is written: "I had a feeling that the red deck will provide the answer."

The volunteer is now asked to take the card case of the red deck, open it, and place the deck face down on the table. Using his index finger, the performer ribbon spreads the cards from left to right. There, in approximately the middle of the red backed cards, is one card with a blue back. The performer asks the volunteer to turn the card over. It is the Eight of Hearts!! This is very surprising, as the deck had previously been shown to contain only red-backed cards.

Method

This is a presentation that again focuses on forcing a known card. The card to be forced, in this example, is the Eight of Hearts; the final card forced is at the discretion of the performer. I believe this presentation is straightforward, convincing, and does away with difficult sleight of hand moves. The set-up for the effect is simple and direct. After introducing the decks, the volunteer is asked to pick either the red or blue deck.

A simple "magician's choice" is used at this point. If the volunteer picks the blue deck, they are asked to place the blue deck in their pocket while the performer shows the volunteer that the face cards of the red deck are different with all cards having red backs. If the volunteer picks the red deck, the performer immediately opens the red deck and demonstrates that the face cards of the deck are different with all cards having red backs. The cards are put back in their case and placed on the table.

The performer now takes the blue deck and, after demonstrating that the face cards are all different and all having blue backs, proceeds to force the Eight of Hearts using any method of their choice. The card is noted by the volunteer, and an additional audience member if possible, and returned to the deck. The deck is thoroughly shuffled by the performer, put back in its case, and placed on the table.

The performer now takes the small piece of paper from his pocket and requests the volunteer to concentrate on the chosen card. The performer writes: "I had a premonition that the red deck will provide the answer" on the paper, folding the same several times, and places it on the table. The performer now asked to identify the chosen card, in this instance, the Eight of Hearts. The paper is opened and the message is revealed. The performer is now takes the red deck from its case and places it face down on the table. Using his index finger, the performer ribbon spreads the cards from left to right. There, in approximately the middle of the red-backed cards, is one card with a blue back. The performer asks the volunteer to turn the card over. It is the Eight of Hearts!!

The preparation of the red deck, containing the one blue-backed force card, is as follows. A duplicate card, a blue-backed Eight of Hearts, is placed three to four cards down from the top of the deck. When the performer fans the deck from his right hand to his left, he demonstrates that all of the cards are, in fact, different. As he turns the deck over and begins spreading them to show their backs are all red, the top five to seven cards are pushed off as a group taking care not to show that one blue deck card is within the first five to seven red-backed cards. The remainder of the cards is shown demonstrating that the backs of all cards are red. The deck is now shuffled, taking care not to "flash" the blue-backed card, which is still positioned in the top five to seven cards. One final cut is made such that the blue-backed card is near the middle of the deck. This is accomplished during the final cut by removing the bottom half of the deck and placing it onto the top half of the deck.

There are many variations of this effect. In one presentation the chosen card is signed by the volunteer and various methods are used to remove the card from one pack and place within the other. This presentation is clean in that no difficult sleight-of-hand is required. Cards are not destroyed with signatures (I am basically frugal and hate to waste cards) and the decks can be used for an extended period of time. In another presentation the force card can be "palmed" from the blue deck while replacing the deck in its card case and placed in the performer's coat pocket. At the conclusion of the effect, the performer can be asked to look through the blue pack of cards to verify that the Eight of Hearts is not there. Although any of these additional steps can be added, the basic effect is strong and can certainly stand alone.

Materials Needed

The performer must have a red and blue back deck of cards, as well as a duplicate, blue-backed, Eight of Hearts.

Additional Scenario

If the performer wishes, the effect can be presented as a prediction. The name of the force card can be written on a sheet of paper and sealed in an envelope. This may be produced prior to beginning the effect and asked to be held by a member of the audience before beginning the routine.

TOSSED OUT DECK

This is a classic of mentalism that has a very positive effect on the audience. Although many credit the popular use of the tossed-out deck to David Hoy (Dr. Faust), the literature finds the use of a deck of cards in similar presentations as early as 1908. Although various methods / specialty decks can be purchased commercially, it is easy to obtain the necessary cards for constructing the deck necessary for the presentation. The performer has various options with respect to the number of cards ultimately identified. In this basic presentation, the deck used will be a three-way force deck. In Hoy's original presentation a one-way force deck was utilized. Some performers advocate the use of a five-way force deck. The specific deck used is at the discretion of the performer (See **Table 2**). Additionally, several specially gimmicked decks (in addition to the one, three and five-way force decks) are available commercially. This trick is most effective for platform or stage, although used in smaller, more intimate gatherings can still be quite effective. Please see the following descriptions for the various basic deck options available to the performer:

Table 2

Type of Force Deck	Cards needed, and order of cards, in the deck*
One-way Deck	All 51 cards are the same with an indifferent card on the face of the deck. Example: 51 cards are all the 7 of Hearts with an indifferent card is placed on the face of the deck. In this example, the card is a Jack of Clubs.
Three-way Deck	17 cards being the 9 of Clubs, 17 cards being the 4 of Hearts, and 17 cards being the Queen of Spades. The cards are rotated as follows: 9 C – 4 H – Q S - 9 C – 4 H – Q S - 9 C – 4 H – Q S – etc, until all cards are used. Additionally, an indifferent card is placed on the face of the deck. In this example, the card is a Jack of Clubs.
Five-way Deck	10 cards being the 9 of Clubs, 10 cards being the 4 of Hearts, and 10 cards being the Queen of Spades, 10 cards being the 2 of Diamonds, and 10 cards being the King of Clubs. The cards are rotated as follows: 9 C – 4 H – Q S – 2 D - K C - 9 C – 4 H – Q S – 2 D - K C - 9 C – 4 H – Q S – 2 D - K C – etc., until all cards are used. Additionally, an indifferent card is placed on the face of the deck. In this example, the card is a Jack of Clubs.

* These are example cards that can be used. The specific cards used are at the discretion of the performer.

Presentation (Using a Three-way forcing deck)

The performer begins this experiment with a general discussion of **Telepathy**, the ability to transfer thoughts or feelings from the mind of one individual to that of another without using the ordinary five senses. The performer produces a deck of cards that is tightly bound by a thick rubber band around the middle of the deck. The performer requests that three volunteers in the audience (one on the far left of the audience, one in the middle, and one on the far right of the audience) will be asked to "peek" at a card, anywhere in the deck, and remember the same. The performer demonstrates the process of the "peek" stressing that only one card is to be identified. The three volunteers are asked to stand and remain standing. The performer then tosses the deck to the individual on the far left of the audience and asks them to "peek" at a card. He then asks that once the first individual has identified a card, the deck be passed to a second individual, on their left, and they also "peek" at a card. The deck is again passed to a third individual, on their left, and the "peek" is repeated one final time. A total of three individuals will have "peeked" at a card at the conclusion of the process. Once the three individuals have identified a card, the deck is tossed back to the performer (If the performer wishes, he can miss catching the deck; this often produces a nice laugh from the audience!).

The performer takes a notepad from his table and asks the three volunteers to concentrate intently on their cards. Several notations are made by the performer on the notepad. After a period of time of intense concentration by the performer, three cards are rapidly named. In this example, the named cards are the Nine of Clubs, Four of Hearts and the Queen of Spades. The performer asks the individuals who are standing if their card was named and, if so, to please sit down. To the amazement and delight of the audience, all three individuals take their seat. The performer receives a well-deserved round of applause!

Method

This effect is accomplished by using a force deck. In this example, a three-way force deck is used. For example, 17 Nine of Clubs, 17 Four of Hearts and 17 Queen of Spades will be alternated to construct a deck of cards (see description above). An indifferent card, for example the Jack of Clubs, is placed face up at the end of the deck completing a three-way force deck. A substantial rubber band is placed around the middle the deck such that if held in an individual's left hand, the right hand can make a break somewhere in the deck and quickly "peek" at a card. This process is demonstrated by the performer indicating that only one card is to be chosen. The deck is then tossed to an individual on the performer's far left and the process of obtaining the identity of the three cards, as described above, is completed.

The performer produces a notepad and asks the three individuals to concentrate intently on their respective cards. Several notations are made (and partially erased for effect!) on the notepad. After a period of time of intense concentration by the performer, the three cards are named. At this time the performer asks them to sit down if their card has been named. To the amazement and delight of the audience, all three volunteers take their seat!

Special Precautions

As a safety factor, the performer can lightly write the names of the three force cards (as well as the cover card) in pencil on the first sheet of the notepad. This allows the performer to concentrate on presentation and not on remembering the three force cards.

In the rare instance that a volunteer does not sit down after the performer has identified the three force cards, one can assume that the individual choose the Jack of Clubs cover card. If this should happen, a Jumbo-sized Jack of Clubs (5 by 7-inch Bicycle Jumbo Card) can be produced from the performer's inside coat pocket (or a sealed 8 by 10-inch manila envelope taped to the performer's table leg). The performer can then ask the individual if this was their chosen card. Unfortunately, some individuals will choose the Jack of Clubs in an effort to cause the performer to fail. Sad, but true!

By requesting the assistance of three well-dispersed audience members (one on the far left, one in the middle, and one on the far right of the audience), the performer can reduce the chance that the individuals know each other personally and not talk to each other at the conclusion of the performance. In rare instances the three individuals may compare their chosen cards and find that one or more did choose the same card. By spacing the individuals throughout the audience during this presentation, the chance of this happening is reduced.

CELL PHONE PREDICTION

This is an impromptu effect that is available to the performer at a moment's notice. Properly presented, the results are quite dramatic.

Effect

The mentalist begins the routine by expressing his anxiety in receiving too many cell phone calls during the day providing a constant interruption to his schedule. To break the monotony of his busy day, he offers a brief demonstration of his mental abilities to several friends gathered around him. He provides a deck of cards (or borrows a deck if one is available), shuffles them thoroughly, and asks for a volunteer to help him in his demonstration. A volunteer is identified and asked to again shuffle the deck and return them to the performer. The performer then asks the volunteer to randomly select a card from the deck (in this example the chosen card was the King of Clubs). This card is seen by the volunteer and several individuals close to him, and returned to the deck. The performer puts the deck into its case and places it on the table in front of him. The volunteer is asked to concentrate on the card.

The performer concentrates intently, but has difficulty in identifying the correct card. Although several attempts are made to identify the card, each attempt fails. Suddenly, the performer's cell phone rings. Irritated, the performer removes the cell phone from his pocket, stops the ringing, and places it next to the deck of cards on the table.

The performer indicates that he needs help in identifying the correct card. Frustrated, the performer asks the volunteer if he would mind if he answered the phone. The performer opens the phone and finds a picture of the King of Clubs card on the screen. He hands the cell phone to the volunteer and asks if the King of Clubs was the card he chose. To the delight of the individuals present, the volunteer indicates that his chosen card was the King of Clubs!

Method

The basis of this effect is to "force" the King of Clubs card on the volunteer. Most, if not all, cell phones today have the ability to take and store pictures in their memory. I would suggest taking pictures of the Queen of Hearts (for female volunteers) and the King of Clubs (for male volunteers) and store in the cell phones "My Pictures" memory section. Prior to beginning the routine, the performer can discretely "save" whichever card needed to the cell phone's "Main Screen/Wallpaper" screen (usually the inside screen of the phone). The final step is to set one of the cell phone's alarm timers to a time approximately two to three minutes from beginning the routine. If the alarm rings earlier than needed during the routine, the performer can simply stop the alarm and place the cell phone down. Experience will help you in timing the routine.

Please consider this effect! It is impromptu and ready at any time. When are you ever without your cell phone? I have been amazed at the spectators' reaction when the card is identified.

CARD CALLING

Although this presentation is not strictly a mentalism effect, it does demonstrate the performer's ability to instantly memorize a randomly selected number of cards obtained from a thoroughly shuffled deck of playing cards. Many individuals have advocated different methods to accomplish this effect including George Sands, Richard Osterland, Bob Cassidy and others. Some methods require considerable card expertise. The basic method used here is credited to George Sands and uses a stripper deck to obtain a memorized set of cards (approximately one-half) from the deck. The cards "memorized" in this presentation are only an example of possible cards to be used. The final selection of cards to be used are at the discretion of the performer. In reality, it should not take more than 2 to 3 hours to memorize the section of cards the performer will ultimately use. It is well worth the time needed to memorize the cards used in this presentation. This is a killer effect that uses one Stripper Deck and provides 8 to 10 minutes of solid entertainment. It can be presented to a small group of individuals or as a stage effect with hundreds in the audience!

Presentation

The mentalist begins his presentation by talking about ways in which one can maintain and improve one's memory, especially as they age. Keeping the mind active, as research on ageing has reported, is important in maintaining and improving one's memory. Many methods to improve memory have been developed and the performer is going to demonstrate a method that has been especially beneficial to him. What makes this presentation interesting for audience members is that the performer is going to explain, in detail, how he is going to accomplish the effect.

The performer asks for two volunteers from the audience who enjoys gambling and are familiar with a deck of playing cards. Once the individuals have been identified and are on stage, one standing on the performer's left and the other on the performer's right, a deck of cards is taken from his coat pocket. The cards are removed from the case and shown to both volunteers noting that it is a regular deck of cards. The performer asks both volunteers to cut the cards several times and return the deck to the performer. He then thoroughly shuffles the cards, again showing their random sequence to the volunteers, cuts the deck approximately in half, and hands one half of the deck to the performer on his left.

The performer states that he is only going to memorize one half of the deck in this presentation to save time. If the card is not in the memorized packet of cards, it is obviously in the other volunteer's pack. The performer then asks if someone in the audience has a watch with a second hand and to please time him as he memorizes the cards in the half of the deck in his possession. The performer asks the audience member to start timing him as he begins to intently concentrate on each card as he spreads them from his right to left hand. After approximately 30 seconds, the performer announces that he has accomplished his goal. The performer then hands the memorized portion of the deck to the volunteer on his right. He asks that both volunteers go through their parts of the deck and place all cards together in the same suit in order from lowest to highest card within each suit. He explains that this will facilitate the demonstration as it unfolds. While the volunteers are arranging their cards, the performer explains to the audience the method he has used to memorize the cards. An example of this process follows:

The performer indicates that he always begins with the Club suit in that a Club represents, for him, an instrument for conflict / battle. If the performer sees the Two of Clubs in the cards being memorized, he "visually" writes on the side of a helium-filled balloon the name of a childhood friend that he often roughhoused (a minor conflict). A string is attached to the balloon and floats above him during his visualization. This is repeated for higher cards within the Club suit representing more aggressive opponents he has experienced as the cards are higher in value (examples: Five of Clubs, name of rival to first girlfriend; Ten of Clubs, interviewing for first job; Ace of Clubs, Adolph Hitler, etc.). This process is repeated for the Diamond (wealth / money factors), Heart (relationship / love factors) and Spade (building / construction factors) suits. At the conclusion of the process, in the mind of the performer, there are approximately 26 balloons "floating around" in front of him with the names of individuals / events written on their sides. Once the card is identified, the performer mentally "bursts the balloon", thus removing it from the remaining cards available. This process is completed when all balloons are destroyed. The performer tells the volunteers that he will point to them while calling out the name of a card they are holding. If the performer is correct, the volunteer is instructed to remove the card and let it fall to the floor. The performer now turns his back to the volunteers and faces the audience.

The performer concentrates and points to the volunteer on his left (the performer's back is now toward the two volunteers) and asks if he holds the Two of Clubs. The volunteer indicates he has the card and drops it to the floor. The performer then points to the volunteer on his right and asks if he has the Three, Four and Five of Clubs. The volunteer on the performer's right acknowledges that he does have the named cards and drops each to the floor. This process is repeated for the remaining Club cards. The performer then proceeds to the Diamond suit and successfully names and identifies the volunteer holding each card in the suit. The process is then completed, with increasing speed, for the Heart and Spade Suits. At the conclusion of the presentation, all 52 cards have been named correctly and are lying on the stage floor. The performer acknowledges the help of his two volunteers, escorts them to the edge of the stage, and takes a well-deserved bow!

Method

As indicated above, a stripper deck is used to accomplish this dramatic demonstration of card memorization. **Table 3** gives a detailed list of all cards within each respective suit and within the set of cards held by each of the two volunteers. It should again be noted that the final cards within each volunteer's pack of cards are at the discretion of the performer. The cards listed in Table 3 are only examples and can be adjusted to each performer's specific preference. It is important that about one half of the deck (26 cards) should be in each pack of the deck.

To begin the effect, the deck of stripper cards is removed from its case and casually shuffled (don't be to fancy; a simple overhand shuffle is best!). The memorized cards are oriented opposite the indifferent cards. The performer can ask one of the volunteers to cut one half of the deck from the performer's right hand into his left hand. A brief shuffle can then be done by the performer with the other volunteer asked to also complete an additional cut as the previous volunteer has done. This is safe handling of the deck in that volunteers never really have full control of the deck, which reduces the chance of the deck being accidentally dropped to the floor (bad move!). It also demonstrates to the audience that the cards are actually being mixed with the aid of both volunteers. The performer can again shuffle the cards ending with a final cut of the cards. This final cut separates the memorized cards from the indifferent cards. Once the cards are cut into two packs the performer hands one pack to one volunteer while he retains the other pack of cards for himself. In this example, there are 24 indifferent cards in one pack and 28 memorized cards in the second pack. These packs easily differ to touch once separated and the performer can give the indifferent pack of cards to the volunteer of his choice. Once the cards are separated, the performer apparently "memorizes" the cards in his pack and the effect can proceed as noted above.

What makes this presentation especially impressive for the audience is the pace at which the performer identifies specific cards in his memorized pack. By pointing to the volunteer to his left and right while naming individual cards, with the cards falling to the floor, a great deal of "activity" happens on the stage.

Table 3

INSTRUCTIONS FOR CARD CALLING POSITIONS

I.   **Performer faces audience with volunteers to his/her back.**

II. **Performer begins with Two of Clubs and follows in sequence listed. As each card is called, the performer points to either the left or right.**

III. **This process is completed, in order, for the Diamond, Heart and Spade suits.**

PERFORMER: Facing the Audience

PERFORMER POSITION	STAGE LEFT						STAGE RIGHT						
CARDS IN PACK													
CLUBS	2	6	7	10	K	A	3	4	5	8	9	J	Q
DIAMONDS	2	3	6	9	J	A	4	5	7	8	10	Q	K
HEARTS	4	6	7	10	J	Q	2	3	5	8	9	K	A
SPADES	2	3	7	8	J	K	4	5	6	9	10	Q	A

Materials Needed

The performer requires a Stripper Deck. Contact your local Magic Dealer or Google "Magicians Stripper Deck".

A very special "Extra Sensational Perception Deck" is available at http://alansands.com. This deck is specially designed for the Memorized Deck and is well adapted to accomplish this effect, allowing volunteers to freely shuffle the deck of cards during the performance.

Additional Thoughts

In the unlikely event you should drop the deck during the performance, you should have a duplicate deck available. You can tell the audience that they are soiled and you require a fresh deck to present the effect (a nice "out").

CHAPTER THREE
Force Numbers For Mentalism Effects

The ability to force specific numbers is important for a multitude of mentalism effects. There are numerous popular force numbers found in the literature. The following are several numbers that are easy to force and have many useful applications in a variety of mentalism effects that require the mentalist to already know a piece of information ("one ahead method", etc.). Many of these methods will be used with effects presented in this book.

Force Numbers 1089 and/or 18

This is a classic, and very well documented, method for forcing the number 1089 and / or 18.

Force number 1089

Ask a volunteer to write on a notepad a number of three different digits, between 300 and 900, making sure you cannot see the number. Ask them to reverse the number and **subtract the smaller of the two numbers from the larger number.** Now have them reverse the new subtracted number and add the two numbers together. The resultant number will be 1089.

Here are some examples:

Example 1	If the first number is larger than the reversed number. 845 - 548 = 297 + 792 = 1089
Example 2	If the reversed number is larger than the first number. First number is 298 and the reversed number is 892 892 − 298 = 594 594 + 495 = 1089

Worst case scenario:

Although the chance of the initial number chosen will yield the desired result is good, not every initial three digit number will work (examples: initial number of 302, 546 and others where the first and third digits differ by only 1 number). This is why you will want to limit the choices of their initial three digit number. Initially, instruct the volunteer to use an initial three digit number, with all three digits different from 300 to 900. A solution to a number below 100 for the first subtraction (302 − 203 = 99) would be to make sure you instruct the volunteer that you need a three digit numbers to complete the calculation. Instruct him to place a zero in the hundreds position to have a three digit number. Tell him that if the total of the first subtraction is say 99, make the number 099. Therefore, 099 + 990 = 1089. You can use any qualifying range you feel appropriate or none at all (if you feel lucky!!).

Force number 18

After completing the above calculation, and before your volunteer tells you the number they have obtained, you can ask your volunteer add the 4 numbers together **(1 + 0 + 8 + 9 = 18).**

Force a number that is twice the current year (If the current year is 2010 the force number would be 4020)

In this example, especially if the volunteer is female, assure her that only she will see what she is writing and that you are only going to ask for a final number!! Give her a notepad and ask her to write down the following numbers ready to be added together.

1. In what year were you born?

2. How many years have you been married?

3. What will be your age at the end of this year?

4. In what year were you married?

Now instruct her to add the four numbers to reach a total. The total will be equal to **TWICE** the current year.

Example 1	In what year were you born?	Answer	1954
In this example the year is **2009** and your volunteer is a married female.	How many years have you been married?	Answer:	33
	What will be your age at the end of this year (12/31/2009)?	Answer:	55
	In what year were you married?	Answer:	1976
	TOTAL 4018		
	If the current year is 2009 X 2 = 4018!		

Additionally, other significant events can be used for this method instead of year and length of marriage (there are many individuals with multiple marriages!!). These events can include the birth of a first child, years in a current job, etc.

Example 2	In what year were you born?	Answer:	1950
In this example the year is **2010** and your volunteer is male.	How old is your oldest child	Answer:	26
	What will be your age at the end of this year (12/31/2010)?	Answer:	60
	In what year was your oldest child born?	Answer:	1984
	TOTAL 4020		
	If the current year is 2010 X 2 = 4020!!		

Worst case scenario

Although you hope the volunteer will record the correct numbers to the questions asked (and their math skills are correct), there is always the possibility that the performers number will not exactly match the volunteer's number. It happens and not to worry!! In your final use of the number obtained, in many instances, being "almost correct" is often as powerful as identifying the exact number. In any instance, the final number obtained should be close to twice the total of the present year. This can be used as a "force number" for many mentalism effects.

IMPROMPTU MATHEMATICAL PRECOGNITION (IMP Experiment)

This presentation is impromptu, straightforward, involves multiple audience members, and will leave a lasting impression of your abilities. This routine can be presented to a group of four to six individuals, although a larger group (stage presentation) can certainty be considered.

Performance

The mentalist begins with a brief discussion of *precognition*, the ability to foresee events through extrasensory means before they happen. This ability, considered by many to be the most significant of all areas of mentalism, occurs most often (up to 70 percent) while dreaming. In fact, the performer tells his audience he had a dream last night about time spent with individuals here this evening. He would like, with their permission, to test the information he saw in his dream. All present agree to his request.

A notepad (small group) or Dry Eraser Board (larger group) is produced and the performer asks a member of the group to name a number from 1 to 9, which is written at the top of the blank page / board. This is repeated with three different individuals until a random 4 digit number is obtained. The performer looks intently at the number, picks up an index card, and writes some information on the card which is not shared with the audience. The card is then placed and sealed in an empty envelope, and placed on a table in full view of the audience.

The following information (example) has been now obtained:

Line 1	6 3 8 3 (obtained by 4 different spectators)

At this time, a volunteer is asked to place a random 3-digit number under the first number. The performer then places a random 3-digit number under the previous spectator's number. Another volunteer then places a random 3-digit number under the performer's number. The performer now places the final random 3-digit number under the previous spectator's number. Finally, the notepad is given to a new spectator to total the numbers, arriving at a grand total.

At this time, the following information (example) has been obtained:

Line 1	6 3 8 3 (obtained by 4 different volunteers)
Line 2	5 6 1 (written by volunteer 1)
Line 3	4 3 8 (written by performer)
Line 4	7 2 6 (written by volunteer 2)
Line 5	2 7 3 (written by performer)
TOTAL	**8 3 8 1** (totaled by volunteer 3)

The performer now asks a volunteer to pick up the sealed envelope, open it and remove the folded index card. He is then asked to read to the audience what is written on the card. The spectator does so and the number written on the card is **8381**.

Method

Although full of audience interaction, the methods used to accomplish this impressive demonstration of precognition is simple to accomplish. The specific steps are as follows:

Once the initial 4-digit number is written on the notepad/board, the performer needs to add 2 to the first number and subtract 2 from the last number, the middle two numbers stay the same.

Examples	6 3 8 3 will be recorded as 8 3 8 1
	7 5 2 6 will be recorded as 9 5 2 4
	8 3 7 0 will be recorded as 10 3 6 8
	9 6 3 1 will be recorded as 11 6 2 9

Note in the last two examples (8370 and 9631) how the first and last numbers are affected by adding 2 and subtracting 2 to the first and last numbers.

After the new number is identified, the performer writes the number on an index card, folds it several times, seals it in an envelope and places it on the table in full view of the audience.

After volunteer 1 has recorded the second number (Line 2), the performer adds the third number making sure that the values for each digit add to 9 (Line 3). This is repeated for volunteer 2 (Line 4) and the performer's next number (Line 5). See the following example:

Line 2	5 6 1 (written by volunteer 1)
Line 3	4 3 8 (written by performer)
	9 9 9 (totals equal 9 in each column)
Line 4	7 2 6 (written by volunteer 2)
Line 5	2 7 3 (written by performer)
	9 9 9 (totals equal 9 in each column)
TOTAL (Lines 2, 3, 4, and 5)	**8 3 8 1** (totaled by volunteer 3)

All that is left to complete the effect is to have the figures totaled and shown to the audience. Have the prediction card unfolded showing that both numbers match exactly! Don't forget to take a well-deserved bow.

CHAPTER FOUR
Bank Note Revelation

The ability of a mentalist to "divine" a serial number of a bank note has long been popular with audiences and a valuable addition to the mentalist's repertoire. It requires little in the way of preparation and has tremendous impact on the audience. Although many methods have been developed to accomplish the effect, the following has proven very effective and has good audience appeal.

Presentation

The performer asks for a volunteer to help him with an experiment in *telepathy*: the psychic phenomena by which communication occurs via mind-to-mind communication. Several members of the audience are asked to provide a dollar bill to be used in the experiment (about five total). The performer requests that all bills be placed face down in the first volunteer's hand so no identifying information can be obtained from the front of each bill. The first volunteer is asked to pick one bill, making sure not to look at the front of the bill, and return the remaining bills to their owners. The volunteer is instructed to fold the front of the bill in half, left to right, and to repeat this process once more left to right. The bill is then again folded; top half folded over the bottom half. The performer now takes the folded bill into his left palm, walks to the other side of the audience, and hands the folded bill to another volunteer. This new volunteer is requested to hold the bill tightly in their hand. The performer then tells the audience that each dollar bill has an eight-digit serial number with letters at the beginning and end of the serial number. Each number series is different and unique to each individual bill. At no time was the serial number seen by either volunteer initially obtaining or folding the bill, the additional volunteer now holding the folded dollar bill, or the performer.

The performer, picking up a note pad from the adjacent table, asks the volunteer to open the folded bill and concentrate on the first letter(s) of the serial number. The first four numbers are asked to be visualized in the volunteer's mind followed by the last four numbers. Finally, the letter(s) at the end of the number series is asked to be visualized.

The performer has been making notes on the notepad during the above process. The performer states that he is having difficulty and asks if the eighth number in the series is either a 7 or 8. The volunteer acknowledges that the eighth number is, in fact, one of the two numbers mentioned. The performer now tears the page from the notepad and hands it to an individual in the audience. The volunteer with the bill is now asked to read the number, one letter and digit at a time, so the individual who has the performer's prediction can verify each as they are identified. This is done with an exact match of all letters and numbers of the serial number on the dollar bill. At this time, the dollar bill is returned to its original owner and the performer takes a well-deserved bow.

Materials Needed

In this presentation the use of a small notepad, thumb tip, and a duplicate dollar bill with the serial number known to the performer are required.

Method

Several factors are important in this presentation to assure smooth working. Many performers recommend using a bill of greater value, usually in the $20-$50 range. Unfortunately, bills in the $5, $10, $20 and $50 range (at the time of this writing) have several different series in circulation among their own respective values. This is not true for the one-dollar bill and, although not potentially as dramatic as when using a higher-denomination bill in the routine, still provides an excellent outcome. The process of collecting several dollar bills from different individuals allows the appearance of a truly independent choice for the selected bill eventually used.

To accomplish the switch of the volunteer's dollar bill for the bill that the performer will provide centers on the use of the venerable thumb tip. Prior to the performance, the performer has obtained a dollar bill that has obvious wear and tear, and is consistent in appearance with other similar dollar bills that will be collected from the various audience members. As the performer is instructing the volunteer to fold the bill, the performer can obtain the thumb tip (with the duplicate bill inside) from his coat or pants pocket. The performer walks toward the audience to obtain the volunteer's folded bill, which is placed into the palm of his left hand. The volunteer should be on the performer's right.

The performer takes the bill into his palm and walks to his left, placing his right thumb (with the thumb tip in place and containing the performer's bill with the known serial number) over the bill in his left palm. As his fingers curl around the bill (and thumb tip), he removes the bill within the thumb tip and turns his left palm away from the audience, walking toward the next volunteer he is going to apparently give the original bill. This transfer is accomplished in natural movement with little attention directed toward the dollar bill in transit. As the performer hands the bill to the new volunteer with his right hand, the thumb tip and the original bill (in his left hand) is discretely deposited into his left coat or pants pocket.

At this time, the notepad is picked up from the performer's table and opened to a "blank page" (remember, the full serial number is already lightly written on the page, just visible enough to allow the performer to read, but not be seen by an audience member). During the process of "visualizing the number in the volunteer's mind", the performer can boldly trace the number over the lighter one already on the page.

After "recording" the serial number, the performer tears the top page off the notepad, folds it several times, and hands it to another individual in the audience. From this point, the presentation comes to a conclusion with the volunteer holding the substituted bill reading each letter and number, one at a time, and verified by the individual with the performer's prediction.

CHAPTER FIVE
Mental Trip Of A Lifetime

Precognition, the act of knowing beforehand that an event will occur, will be the focus of this demonstration. One of the most popular prediction methods, popularized by U.S. Grant, is the Mental Epic. Many variations have appeared in the literature and on the market. The effect is based on the "one ahead method" in which one of three predications to be made is already known by the performer. The effect generally requires a rather large gimmicked board (suitable for larger audiences), which often suggests to the audience the possibility of a "magic trick" rather than a demonstration of the performer's mental ability.

In this more impromptu presentation, the use of readily available materials are advocated; in this example a spiral bound note pad, pencil and a bit of showmanship. Basically, the effect involves three individual predictions that are blended into one central theme. Any theme the performer would like to use is certainly acceptable. The following presentation uses the "one ahead method" in which the performer has previously obtained one of the three predictions to be made.

Presentation

The mentalist begins with a brief discussion of precognition (performer's discretion as to length, detail, etc.). An audience volunteer is asked to help the performer in taking a Mental Trip of a Lifetime. The performer takes a note pad from his table and asks the volunteer the following three questions:

1. What country would you most like to visit on this make-believe trip?

Before the volunteer announces his answer, the performer concentrates and writes his prediction on the first page of the note pad, tears it from the pad, folds it several times and places it on the table. The volunteer is asked to identify to the audience the name of the country. He does so.

The performer then asks the second question:

2. While in the country, what special activity would you like to do (climb a mountain, surf, etc., the activity is totally up to the volunteer)?

Before the volunteer announces his answer, the performer concentrates and writes his prediction on the second page of the note pad, tears it from the pad, folds it several times, and places it on the table. The volunteer is asked to identify to the audience the activity. He does so.

The performer then asks the third and final question:

3. How much money would be you need to make this trip possible?

Before the volunteer announces his answer, the performer concentrates and writes his prediction on the third page of the note pad, tears it from the pad, folds it several times and places it on the table. The volunteer is asked to identify to the audience the amount of money. He does so.

At this time the performer gathers all three predictions and asks the volunteer to review the country he would like to visit, the activity he would like to do while in the country, and the amount of money he would need to make the trip possible. In this example the responses given were: Germany, attend Oktoberfest in Berlin, and $5,445.00.

The performer opens his first prediction and shows he has written "Germany" on the paper, the second paper reveals "Attend Oktoberfest in Berlin", and the third prediction has "$5,400.00". All three predictions made by the performer were amazingly accurate! The performer now takes a well-deserved round of applause.

Method

The major objective the performer must accomplish prior to beginning this presentation is to force the dollar amount on the future volunteer without his knowledge. An individual is asked, prior to the performance, if he would help the performer with an experiment that evening. The individual is told that during the performance he will be asked some questions concerning a fictitious trip and he will need to have some money to take the trip. The performer would like to identify an amount of money that neither he, nor the individual, has any idea of what the final amount will be. Thus, a "free choice" will be assured in arriving at the final dollar amount.

The performer proceeds with the "1089" number force (or any other number force the performer feels appropriate: see Chapter 3). Once the individual has obtained the number 1089 (this number is apparently not known to the performer), the volunteer is asked if the amount, in dollars, would be sufficient for the anticipated trip? Most likely, the answer will be "No". The performer then asks the volunteer to multiply the number by 5 to obtain a more appropriate dollar amount for the trip ($1,089 X 5 = $5,445.00). The performer emphasizes that the dollar amount was identified through a totally random process and that the performer does not know the final figure. The volunteer is asked to keep the paper that the dollar amount is recorded and to use this amount during the performance when asked to provide the amount for the trip. The volunteer is told that this will save time during the performance (also ensuring the force number will be used).

At the beginning of the presentation the performer asks the volunteer who has the predetermined dollar amount to help him with an experiment in precognition. The volunteer is invited on stage and stands next the performer with a small table between them.

To begin the routine the performer asks the volunteer a country that he would like to visit. As described above, and prior to the volunteer announcing his choice, the performer writes the dollar amount of $5,400.00 on the first page of the note pad, tears it from the pad, folds it several times and places it on the table. Note that what is written by the performer on the paper **WAS NOT** the country, but rather that the **DOLLAR AMOUNT NEEDED** for the anticipated trip. Also note that the dollar amount the performer has written is not exactly that of the volunteer. "Almost correct" can often be more convincing than exactly correct!! At this time the volunteer is asked to announce the country which, from the audience perspective, the performer has already recorded before being announced by the volunteer.

The performer now asks the volunteer for an activity he would like to do while in that country. As before, and prior to the volunteer announcing the activity, the performer writes the **NAME OF THE COUNTRY** on the second page of the note pad, tears it from the pad, folds it several times, and places it on the table. From the audience perspective the performer has recorded the activity when in truth, the name of the country has been written.

For the last prediction, the performer asks the volunteer the dollar amount he would need to complete the trip. The performer can quietly ask the volunteer to use the figure he has already determined. This is done in a very subtle way and should not be noticed by the audience. As above, the performer writes the **NAME OF THE ACTIVITY** on the third page of the note pad, tears it from the pad, folds it several times, and places it on the table. From the audience perspective, the performer is recording the dollar amount when, in fact, he is recording the activity the volunteer would like to accomplish while in the country. The performer now takes the three predictions in his right hand and reviews the three questions, with the volunteer's responses, with the audience. In this example, the country was Germany, the activity was attending Oktoberfest in Berlin, and the dollar amount needed to finance the trip was $5,445.00. While the volunteer is confirming his answers, the performer is opening all three predictions and placing them, one at a time (and apparently in order of them being identified), face down on the table. The performer now gives the three predictions to an audience member close to him and asks them to read aloud the three predictions. All three predictions made by the performer were amazingly accurate!

Some performers may be concerned that the predictions were placed on the table and left in sequence order as revealed by the performer. As stated before, while the performer is confirming the country, the activity, and the dollar amount, he is casually opening each prediction and placing them face down on the table. If this is done in a natural and nonchalant manner, little attention will be drawn to the process.

Other Thoughts

Of course, any theme can be used for this presentation. An important aspect is to use one that you find interesting and can relate. An example includes:

A Trip to Las Vegas (using a card force to obtain one of the three predictions needed): You could use a deck of cards and force the Queen of Hearts on a female volunteer and tell her this is her lucky card for an imaginary trip to Las Vegas. (1) Ask her for a casino she would like to gamble while in Las Vegas? (MGM Grand Casino for this example: performer writes Queen of Hearts). (2) Ask her for a game she would like to play (Roulette in this example: performer writes MGM Grand). (3) Ask her for her lucky card? (Queen of Hearts in this example: performer writes Roulette.

CHAPTER SIX
Drawing Duplication

The duplication of a drawing randomly chosen by a volunteer is a well documented, and very popular, effect of the mentalist's repertoire. Many excellent examples of this effect are documented in the literature, especially those of Annenmann, Richard Osterlind, Max Maven and others. When properly presented, the effect has a devastating impact on the audience. The drawing options presented to the volunteer can be varied. The most important factor for the effect to have maximum impact is that each option for drawing be easily recognized by the volunteer and the members of the audience.

The basis of the effect is that the performer can discreetly identify the drawing chosen by the volunteer or the performer can, in a subtle way, force the choice of the drawing. The former method is used here. The following presentation provides a generic option for the performer. Final choices for potential drawings are left to the discretion of the performer (See Table 4 for sample drawing topics).

Presentation

The mentalist begins this demonstration with a brief discussion of **Clairvoyance,** the paranormal visual acquisition of knowledge about an object, situation, or event (length and detail of discussion per the performer's wishes). To test the performer's clairvoyant ability, a volunteer is asked to join him on stage. The performer picks up a card box from a table, removes a packet of cards, and casually shows them to the volunteer.

The performer announces that the packet contains 26 playing cards. On the face of each card is a white 1" by 2 5/8" mailing label with the name of a different well-known object printed on it (**Table 4**). The performer casually fans the pack of cards face up, names a few, and mentions that all objects on the cards are different. The performer turns the cards face down, shuffles them to assure that they are well mixed, and asks the volunteer to pick any card and remove it from the deck. The volunteer is asked to look at the object printed on the face of the card and show it to one additional audience member close to them (some individuals will, at times, be nervous and forget the object!). The volunteer is requested to return the card face down into the packet. The performer then thoroughly shuffles the packet, places it back into the empty card case, and lays it on the table.

Table 4

LETTER *	ITEM	LETTER	ITEM
A	AIRCRAFT CARRIER	O	OCTOPUS
B	TRICYCLE	P	PALM TREE
C	LOG CABIN	Q	QUILL PEN
D	DASCHUND DOG	R	ROLLER SKATE
E	ELEPHANT	S	RATTLESNAKE
F	FEATHER	T	EIFFEL TOWER
G	GUITAR	U	UMBRELLA
H	TWO-STORY HOUSE	V	VIOLIN
I	IGLOO	W	WITCH
J	JACK O' LANTERN	X	XYLOPHONE
K	RICH KING	Y	YAGHT
L	PRESIDENT LINCOLN	Z	ZEBRA
M	MERMAID	**Note:** Each Item is generally related on a letter of the alphabet. Final choices are at the discretion of the performer.	
N	PEARL NECLACE		

* Generally, each object is associated with the 26 letters of the alphabet.

The performer then gives the volunteer a standard size clipboard, with an 8.5 by 11.0 inch piece of blank white paper clipped to the board and a black magic marker pen. The performer then escorts the volunteer to one end of the stage and asks them to sit down in a chair that is positioned there. The performer walks to his table, upon which is an identical clipboard with a blank white paper attached, and moves to the opposite end of the stage. The performer asks the volunteer to concentrate intently on the object she chose and, to the best of her ability, draw the object on the paper attached to her clipboard. The performer now removes a black magic marker pen from his pocket, concentrates, and also begins to draw.

After a brief time, the performer asks the volunteer if she has completed her drawing. The performer also indicates that he has also completed his drawing. The performer asks the volunteer to hold the drawing tightly against her chest and walk to the center of the stage where she is joined by the performer. The performer then asks the volunteer to turn her drawing towards the audience so all audience members can view it. The performer now shows his drawing, first to the volunteer, without showing it to the audience. This usually elicits a surprised reaction from the volunteer! The performer now turns his drawing towards the audience and, amazingly, both drawings are remarkably similar! A convincing demonstration of clairvoyance!! The performer thanks the volunteer for her participation and escorts her back to her seat in the audience.

Materials

The materials required for this outstanding effect are readily available at minimal cost. The objects for the volunteer to choose are printed on white mailing labels (Label size 1" by 2 5/8": Avery labels 5160/8160) and placed on the face of 26 playing cards. The final objects used are at the discretion of the performer. The pack of cards contains 26 cards (50% of the deck) from a commercially available **stripper deck**. The 26 cards should be randomly assigned to each half of the deck. The performer will now have two packs of prepared cards in case one pack is damaged! When transferring the labels to the face of the cards, care must be taken to make sure that all cards within the pack are oriented the same. This will make "peeking" at the chosen card easier, as detailed later in the presentation.

Method

After showing the volunteer that each card face contains a label printed with a different object, the pack is thoroughly shuffled and the volunteer freely chooses any card within the pack (no force!). While the volunteer is looking at the face of their chosen card, and showing it to an individual close to her for future verification (if needed), the remaining pack can be reversed such that the volunteer's card, once replaced in the pack of cards, can be easily found and shuffled to the top of the pack. The performer then shuffles the pack such that the chosen card is brought to the <u>bottom</u> of the pack. As the performer picks up the empty card case to place the shuffled pack of cards, the performer quickly glimpses at the object on the face of the bottom card. This was the card chosen by the volunteer.

The volunteer is now provided a standard size clipboard, with an 8.5 by 11-inch piece of blank paper clipped to the board, and a black magic marker pen. She is escorted to the far right side of the stage. The volunteer is instructed to concentrate on the object and, to the best of her ability, draw the object on the paper provided. During this time the performer is doing the same at the opposite end of the stage. After a sufficient amount of time has passed for both to complete their respective drawings, both holding their drawings tight against their chests, meet at center stage. Prior to the performer showing his drawing to the audience, he shows it to the volunteer. This action usually elicits a positive reaction from the volunteer and "primes" the audience for the performer's final reveal. The performer then turns his drawing toward the audience so all audience members can see the two drawings. Reaction to the similarities in the drawings is often dramatic.

CHAPTER SEVEN
Book Tests

Book tests have been a staple for the mentalist for many years. In the following description of a "generic" book test, the performer asks for a volunteer, as well as an impartial assistant, to help him in completing a demonstration of ***pre cognition / mindreading*** (depending on the final outcome of the effect you choose). Although there are "gimmicked" books available to the performer to present many book tests, the following rely on regular, non-gimmicked books that can be thoroughly examined by volunteers participating in the routines described below.

Three paperback books are introduced and offered for examination by members of the audience. After verification that the books appear normal, the performer asks the volunteer to select one of the books for further use. The remaining two books are placed aside. The performer now asks the impartial assistant to use an additional paperback book to arrive at a random page number as the performer fans through the pages of the book until instructed by the assistant to stop. The assistant announces the page identified and the performer asks the volunteer to turn to the identified page in the book he is holding. The volunteer is instructed to read the contents of the first complete paragraph on the identified page and to intently concentrate on the words being read. The performer takes a dry erase board and begins to record his impressions of what the volunteer is reading. After several minutes of intense concentration, the performer places the slate down, back to the audience so no writing can be seen, in full view of the audience. The performer now asks the volunteer to read aloud the contents of the paragraph. Upon completion of the reading, the performer turns the dry erase board around revealing a detailed description of the volunteer's reading.

Various methods (perhaps hundreds!) have been used to accomplish this type of book test. The following four book tests, one impromptu and three requiring some preparation, allows the performer a great deal of latitude in their presentation.

Single Book Test

This impromptu book test is always ready to perform using a minimal of materials readily found in a friend's home. The basis of this routine is forcing the number 1089 on the volunteer (see Chapter Three) and using the same to identify a page and line number to identify a mentally pictured word by the volunteer.

Presentation

The performer casually picks up a paperback book found at a friend's home. The performer asks for a volunteer to help him in an experiment in predicting the future! The volunteer is given the chosen book to hold while the next phase of the experiment is completed. The performer now indicates that a random number needs to be determined. The process to obtain the force number 1089 is now completed. The number 1089 has apparently been freely obtained by the volunteer.

The volunteer is asked to open the paperback book to page 108 and go to the 9th line on the page. The volunteer is then instructed to find the longest word on the 9th line and to concentrate only on that one word. The performer removes a sealed envelope from his coat pocket and hands it to another audience member. The performer states "he had a feeling last night" that the contents of the envelope would have meaning this evening. The volunteer is now asked to identify the word. The individual holding the envelope is instructed to open it, remove the piece of paper inside, and read what is written on it. To the amazement of all present, the words match exactly!

Method

Earlier in the evening, the performer discreetly finds a suitable paperback book (typical novel with about 350 to 500 pages) at the host's residence. He turns to page 108 and goes to the 9th line on the page. Usually one word on the line will be longer than the others and will serve the purpose of the experiment. An example of identifying the appropriate word on the 9th line might be as follows:

"When in the room, Bob was jubilant that the coins may be there."

In this instance, the word "jubilant" would be chosen by the performer. Several books may have to be evaluated until a suitable one was identified. This word would now be written on a piece of paper and sealed in an envelope (if used as a *precognitive* effect) or remembered and written on a piece of paper at the conclusion of the book test (if used for a *mindreading* effect). Once the book has been identified, it is placed close (but not too close) to where the impromptu performance will take place. The performer, when the time arrives to select a book, can casually mention that he needs a book and point to the indicated book as a possible candidate for the experiment.

MAGICIAN'S CHOICE / EQUIVOQUE

This is a generic process (with regards to a "typical" book test in the following example) in which the mentalist asks a volunteer to make an apparently free choice among three books. In reality, the performer ends up with a book he wanted the volunteer to choose. This process may be used in a variety of "force" situations (cards, sealed envelopes, etc.).

Method

The performer provides three books for consideration, placing them in a row on a table. For this generic example, the performer ultimately wishes the volunteer to choose the book in the middle. The performer initially asks the volunteer to "take away" any two books (note the performer did not say "choose" any two books). The following choices are available to the volunteer:

1. If the volunteer removes the book on the left and right, the performer takes them and indicates that "we will use the remaining book (the one in the center) in our experiment."

2. If the volunteer removes the center and one indifferent book, the performer asks the volunteer to give him one of the two books. If he hands the performer the indifferent book, the performer finishes the statement "and we will place this book aside." It is important **not to complete the statement** "and we will place this book aside" until it becomes obvious he is handing you the indifferent book. If he hands you the center

book, the performer will say "and we will use this book for our experiment." In either case, the middle book (force book) will be chosen.

THREE-BOOK TEST (Version 1)

Although this book test requires prior preparation, it is very effective, easy to construct and a real audience pleaser. It is especially impressive in that the mentalist describes, in detail, an entire paragraph the volunteer has read in a freely chosen book rather than a single word, as in the previous example. This routine requires the use of the Magician's Choice (see above).

Three paperback books (each book having approximately 350 to 450 pages) are introduced and offered for examination by members of the audience. After verification that the books are normal, the performer asks the volunteer to select one of the books for further use (Magician's Choice). The remaining two books are placed aside.

The performer now asks an impartial assistant to help him identify a random page number to help complete the experiment at hand. An additional paperback book is introduced by the performer. The performer fans the pages for the assistant, stopping at several different pages of the book, demonstrating that each page is different. The performer then fans the pages of the book and requests the assistant to say "stop" anywhere she feels appropriate. She does so and announces the page identified (in this example page 173 is announced to the audience). The performer asks the volunteer to turn to page 173 in the book he has chosen. The volunteer is instructed to read the contents of the first complete paragraph on the identified page and to intently concentrate on the words being read. The performer takes a dry erase board and begins to record his impressions of what the volunteer is reading. After several minutes of intense concentration the performer places the slate down, back showing to the audience so no writing can be seen, in full view of the audience. The performer now asks the volunteer to read aloud the contents of the paragraph. Upon completion of the reading the performer turns the board around revealing a detailed description of the volunteer's reading.

Method

As described previously, the first three paperback books offered for examination to audience members are unprepared. The performer does, however, have detailed knowledge of the facts in the first complete paragraph of book number two (in this example). The performer completes a Magician's Choice leaving book two (the force book) with the volunteer.

The performer now asks the impartial assistant to assist him in identifying a page number to continue the experiment. The performer shows the assistant that the paperback book he has introduced is unprepared. The pages of the book are fanned and the assistant says "stop" at a place they determine. What is not known to the assistant is that a business-size card (or one half of a playing card cut lengthwise) is tightly wedged against the spine of the book, about one inch down from the top edge of the book between pages 172 (left page) and 173 (right page). By practicing fanning the pages several times, it becomes easy to apparently stop at the page indicated when the assistant says 'stop". You may want to try several card sizes to find one that easily stops when indicated by the assistant. The performer needs to turn his head away from the book when the pages are being fanned. Additionally, the book should not be opened too far as to expose the wedged card. Ideally, page numbers should be of large font located in the lower right corner of each page. This should allow the book to only be opened slightly to expose the indicated page number.

Once the page has been announced and the volunteer begins reading the indicted paragraph on that page, the performer can start to record his impressions on the dry erase board (hand-held chalk tablet if a purest!). After an appropriate period of time, the volunteer is asked to read the paragraph to the audience and the performer reveals his predictions to be remarkably the same.

Materials Needed

Four different paperback books with approximately 350 to 450 pages in each book. One 12 inch by 16 inch, white, dry erase board with erasable black marker. Business card/size adjusted playing card.

Additional Scenario

Rather than a **mindreading** effect, the performer can record the contents of the paragraph prior to the performance on a sheet of paper and seal it in an envelope (now a **precognition** effect). The envelope can be placed in full view of the audience throughout the performance. The volunteer reads the paragraph with the envelope opened after the reading. The contents of the envelope matches, in detail, the information provided by the volunteer.

THREE-BOOK TEST (Version 2)

This version is presented the same as Version 1 except the performer has memorized the contents of the first complete paragraph, of all three paperbacks, at the chosen force page. This information can be recorded in pencil, very lightly and in outline form, on the dry erase board (small enough not to be seen by audience members) In this example the Magician's Choice is not required. The performer does need to physically see which book is finally chosen to assure his accurate reproduction of the same.

THREE-YEAR BOOK TEST

This is one routine I really hate to give away. Believe me, get the required materials, do the work necessary, and reap the rewards!!

This is a book test that allows the performer to describe, in detail, an entire paragraph the volunteer has read in a freely chosen book. This routine <u>does not</u> require the use of the Magician's Choice to obtain the selected book.

Four paperback books (each book having approximately 350 to 450 pages) are introduced and offered for examination by four members of the audience. After verification that the books are normal, the performer asks the volunteers to select one of the books for further use. The performer turns his back so he can not see which book is being chosen. The volunteers decide which of them is to hold the chosen book. The chosen book is held behind the back of that volunteer, out of sight of the performer, with the remaining three books placed in a large paper bag, tightly closed and placed aside. The performer emphasizes that he does not know which book was chosen.

Book Tests

The performer now asks an impartial assistant to help him identify a random page number to help complete the experiment at hand. An additional paperback book is introduced by the performer. The performer fans the pages of the book for the assistant, stopping at several different pages of the book, demonstrating that each page is different. The performer then fans the pages of the book and requests the assistant to say "stop" anywhere she feels appropriate. She does so and is asked by the performer if she has identified a page number. She is not to tell anyone the page number EXCEPT the volunteer with the chosen book.

The performer now asks the assistant to go to the volunteer with the chosen book and "whisper" the page number to him. The volunteer is instructed to turn around so the performer cannot see which book he has in his possession. He is requested to read the contents of the first complete paragraph on the page. He is to concentrate intently on the words being read. The performer takes a dry erase board and begins to record his impressions of what the volunteer is reading. After several minutes of intense concentration, the performer places the slate down, back showing so no writing can be seen, in full view of the audience.

The performer now summarizes what has taken place: (1) one of the four books was freely chosen by four volunteers to be used in this presentation. The performer does not know which book was chosen; (2) a random page number was obtained by an independent assistant from an additional book not associated with the original four books; (3) the random page number was secretly told to the volunteer holding the chosen book. The performer does not know what page number was chosen; and (4) the volunteer, out of sight of the performer, has read the first complete paragraph on the chosen page.

The performer now asks the volunteer to read aloud the paragraph. Upon completion of the reading, the performer turns the board around revealing a detailed description of the volunteer's reading. Mindreading at its best!

Method

The four paperbacks required for this effect are listed below. The books are offered for examination to audience members and are all different and unprepared. The titles of the books are:

(1) *Half of a Yellow Sun* (Chimamanda Ngozi Adichie)

(2) *Gramercy Park* (Paula Cohen)

(3) *Rebel* (Bernard Cornwell)

(4) *Communion* (Whitley Strieber)

What is important about each book is that the first complete paragraph on page 135 (the "forced" page number in this routine) in each book has remarkably similar descriptions of a given situation. A "synopsis" of facts found in the four different paragraphs follow:

(1) *Half of a Yellow Sun*: Page 135. Taking a train and watching a bird with a blood red breast perched on the lawn. Two people.

(2) *Gramercy Park*: Page 135. A train speeds, like a comet, along a river, a couple / two passengers.

(3) *Rebel*: A train clanked and hissed, steam billowing, on a bridge along a river with two engineers.

(4) *Communion*: I took a train to Italy. I met a woman and the two of

us began to travel together. We went to Rome and Florence.

As you can see, all paragraphs deal with a train and other materials that are similar in nature. It is important to realize that an <u>exact</u> reproduction of the material being read is not desired. Reading another individual's mind is difficult, and a "close" reproduction is more believable than an exact reproduction. You may want to use any three rather than four books listed for your particular presentation. The decision is up to you and your particular situation. Three years in searching bookstores led me to these four books with similar descriptors within the first complete paragraph on page 135, hence the title *Three-Year Book Test*!

Once the book is chosen by the four volunteers, and the other three books put in a paper bag and placed aside, forcing the page number is accomplished as described in Three Book Test (Version 1: see above). In this instance the assistant does not identify the page number (135 in this example) and is requested to "whisper" the number to the volunteer with the chosen book. The performer already knows the forced page number. Once the page has been told to the volunteer, he begins reading the indicted paragraph on page 135 and the performer can start to record his impressions on the dry erase board. After an appropriate period of time, the volunteer is asked to read the paragraph to the audience and the performer reveals his predictions to be remarkably the same.

Remember, from the audience perspective:

(1) One of the four books was freely chosen by four volunteers to be used in this presentation. The performer does not know which book was chosen; (2) a random page number was obtained by an independent assistant from an additional book not associated with the original four books; and (3) the random page number was secretly told to the volunteer holding the chosen book. The

performer does not know what page number was chosen. (4) The volunteer, out of sight of the performer, has read the first complete paragraph on the chosen page.

Ordering instructions for the four books:

Half of a Yellow Sun by Chimamanda Ngozi Adichie
Paperback Book
Anchor Books @ www.anchorbooks.com
ISBN: 978-1-4000-9520-9

Gramercy Park by Paula Cohen
Paperback Book
St. Martin's Press @ www.stmartins.com
ISBN: 0-312-27552-8 (hc)
ISBN: 0-312-30997-X (pbk)

Rebel by Bernard Cornwell
Paperback Book
HarperCollins Publishers Inc. @ www.harpercollins.com
ISBN: 0-06-093461-I

Communion by Whitley Strieber
Paperback Book
HarperCollins Publishers Inc. @ www.harpercollins.com
ISBN: 978-0-06-147418-7

To find these books: Contact publishers or use www.Amazon.com/ Books and search for respective titles / ISBN numbers.
This is an exceptional routine that is bound to leave the audience in shock!

CHAPTER EIGHT
A Finish To Remember

The following is recommended for the final effect of performances that have been contracted several weeks ahead of the actual event. In preparation for your program (See Chapter Nine), you have put together a varied and interesting program. You have information that will come to light during your presentation (examples: a specific card to be forced, information to be identified during a book test, the serial number of a borrowed dollar bill, etc.) that can be used as "predictions" made by you several weeks prior to your program!

Take a large piece of paper (24 inch by 36 inch) and write "Predictions" in large letters at the top of the paper. First list the card "forced" during the Power of Touch routine, followed by several specific items found in the Three-Year Book Test routine and finally the serial number of the dollar bill used in the Bank Note Revelation routine (these are examples; you can use any information you feel appropriate from the specific routines you use). Fold the paper such that each "prediction" will be shown, one at a time, at the end of the performance. You can fold the paper in a packet and mail it to the host of the performance several weeks prior. Call him and tell him you are mailing a package that relates to your performance. Ask him not to open the package, but be sure to bring it to your show.

When you have finished your performance, ask the individual to join you on stage and to bring the package you mailed him. Ask him to verify the date he received the package (via the cancelled postage stamp on the package) and to verify that he has not opened the package. You can tell the audience that you often have dreams about your performances prior to doing them and that you had a dream about this one several weeks ago. You wrote the information down and mailed it to the host to see if you were correct in your premonition. Now ask the host to open the package and, one at a time, show it to the audience members. The reaction to this process is often quite dramatic and well worth the time and effort involved.

CHAPTER NINE
Putting Together Your Mentalism Program

Now that you have read each chapter of the book you have an idea of the type of effects available as you begin to build a solid, entertaining program. You have a wealth of routines to pick from. Several things are important to remember as you begin the process. Four or five effects (approximately 25 to 30 total minutes), done extremely well and with confidence, is a worthy goal at this, or any stage, in a career. In constructing your overall program consider the following:

1. Vary the type of routines you present. Do not have three "mind reading" effects in your show. You need to vary the presentations to demonstrate the wide range of abilities you have attained (ability to predict the future, mind reading, rapid memorization, etc.) during your study and practice of performance mentalism.

2. It is best to start with an interesting, although not overly dramatic (or difficult) routine. By using a simple, straightforward presentation, you can help deal with any "stage fright" issues you may have and concentrate on presentation. Build to the one routine that floors them!!

3. Make sure you have a written "patter" for every routine you present. Commit it to memory. Knowing the story is

interesting and fits the routine allowing you to concentrate on the presentation.

4. Always have a well-prepared encore routine available to present if asked to do so. Never decline an encore request unless your contract does not allow you to do so.

The following is an example of a solid 20 to 35 minute presentation. The routines listed are only suggestions. Pick those routines that you feel comfortable in performing and use the suggestions listed above. Enjoy!!

Effect	Time Estimate
Pre-talk	(1 – 2 minutes)
The Power of Touch	(3 – 4 minutes)
Three-Year Book Test	(5 – 7 minutes)
Drawing Duplication	(5 – 6 minutes)
Card Calling	(6 – 10 minutes)
Total Time	**(20 – 29 minutes)**

One Encore of Choice (examples)	
Trip to Las Vegas	(5 - 6 minutes)
Predict-a-Number	(3 - 4 minutes)
Tossed Out Deck	(5 – 6 minutes)
Total Time with Encore	**(26 – 35 minutes)**

BUILDING YOUR BOOK AND DVD LIBRARY

The following books and DVD's are only suggestions for those interested in developing an interest in performance mentalism. This is a **BASIC** list! There are many outstanding books and DVD's available for purchase, and should be considered as your interest grows. Many, but not all, of the books are available in paperback at a very reasonable cost. The DVD's are excellent investments in that you see **OUTSTANDING** professionals demonstrate and explain many exciting effects. Cost is a factor in that most DVD's can cost about $30.00 to $35.00 each (package deals are often available from many dealers). You can contact your magic dealer directly, Google the respective title, or go to www.amazon.com

BOOKS

13 Steps to Mentalism, by Corinda
Hardback: 424 pages
Publisher: D. Robins and Co. (1968)
Language: English
ASIN: B00168B6QM

Practical Mental Magic, by Theodore Annemann
Paperback: 320 pages
Publisher: BN Publishing (October 9, 2008)
Language: English
ISBN -10: 1607960044
ISBN – 13: 978-1607960041

Self-Working Mental Magic, by Karl Fulves
Paperback: 127 pages
Publisher: Dover Publications (November 1, 1979)
Language: English
ISBN -10: 0486238067
ISBN – 13: 978-0486238067

Mind, Myth & Magick, by T.A. Waters
Hardbound: 840 pages
Publisher: Hermetic Pr (November 1993)
Language: English
ISBN-10: 094529610X
ISBN-13: 978-0945296102

DVD's

Banachek - Psi Series Volume 1 to 4

Larry Becker - Mental Masterpieces
Larry Becker - Standing Ovation

Bob Cassidy - Mental Miracles

Doc Hilford - Monster Mentalism Volume 1 to 4

Ted Lesley - Cabaret Mindreading

Max Maven - Videomind Volume 1 to 3
Max Maven - Nothing

Richard Osterlind - Mind Mysteries Volume 1 to 7
Richard Osterlind - Easy to Master Mental Miracles Volume 1 to 4
Richard Osterlind - No Camera Tricks

SELECTED GLOSSARY
OF COMMON TERMS
FOR THE PERFORMER *

Billet: A small piece of paper containing a variety of information, which is generally used in the performance of an effect of mentalism.

Book Test: An effect which, in general, a spectator chooses one book (from several offered) and selects a word or sentence on a randomly chosen page. The performer can name the word or provide an impression of what the spectator has read.

Card Force: One of any number of methods used in close-up magic to apparently offer the subject a free or random choice of card when, in fact, the performer knows in advance which card will be chosen. A large variety of card forces exist in which most, but not all, are based on sleight of hand. Forcing a card is often used by the performer in various effects.

Clairaudience: The paranormal auditory acquisition of knowledge; clairaudience often occurs in conjunction with clairvoyance.

Clairvoyance: Often referred to as remote viewing, clairvoyance is the paranormal visual acquisition of knowledge about a contemporary object, situation, or event.

Cold Reading: A series of techniques used by performers, fortunetellers, psychics, and mediums to determine details about another person in order to convince them that the reader knows much more about a subject than he or she actually does.

Déjà vu: The feeling of having already experienced something actually being experienced for the first time.

Equivoque: A technique in which a performer appears to have intended a particular outcome, when in actuality the outcome is one of several alternative outcomes. In a typical example of equivocate (also known as the Magician's Choice), the performer will ask a spectator to make an apparently free choice among several items. No matter what choices the spectator makes, the magician ends up with the item which he wanted the spectator to choose.

ESP (Zener) Cards: A special deck of cards developed by perceptual psychologist Karl Zener for use by J. B. Rhine in tests of extrasensory perception. A standard pack contains 25 cards, each portraying one of five symbols — circle, cross, wavy lines, square or star.

Extra Sensory Perception (ESP): Communication or perception by means other than the five physical senses. Often referred to as "The Sixth Sense".

Hot Reading: The use of foreknowledge when giving a "psychic" reading in mentalism or magic performances, or in other contexts. The reader can gain information about the sitter (person receiving the reading) through a variety of means, such as pre-performance research or overhearing a conversation.

Hypnosis: A trancelike state, artificially induced, in which a person has a heightened suggestibility, and in which suppressed memories may be experienced.

Intuition: The act or faculty of knowing or sensing without the use of rational processes; immediate cognition.

Jumbo Deck: A deck that is four times the size of a standard card deck and is used primarily for stage presentations where regular cards are difficult to see. The use of jumbo cards allows many traditional close-up mentalism effects involving cards to adapt to larger audiences by increased visibility of the cards by audience members.

Latent Telepathy: An instance of telepathy in which there seems to be a time lag between the agent's attempt to transmit the target, and the percipient's awareness of that target.

Mentalism (Performance): A performing art in which its practitioners, known as performers, use mental acuity, cold reading, hot reading, principles of stage magic, and/or suggestion to present the illusion of mind reading, psychokinesis, extra-sensory perception, precognition, clairvoyance or mind control. Hypnosis is also included in this category.

Muscle-reading: A phenomena which mimics telepathy, in which a person is able to find a hidden object by means of physical contact with the person who knows its whereabouts, probably due to subtle muscular cues.

Paranormal: A general term that describes unusual experiences that lack a scientific explanation, or phenomena alleged to be outside of science's current ability to explain or measure.

Precognition: Clairvoyant-like knowledge of future events, objects, or situations. Perception of the past is known as "retrocognition."

Precognitive Telepathy: The paranormal acquisition of information concerning the future mental state of another conscious being.

Premonition: A feeling or impression that something is about to happen, especially something ominous or dire, yet about which no normal information is available.

Pseudo Psychometry: A type of mentalism routine where several spectators have items that are associated with them and the performer somehow identifies which item is owned by which person. In these routines, items are typically borrowed from audience members and mixed as the performer looks away. The performer then brings out each object and identifies its owner.

Psychometry: A form of extra-sensory perception in which a psychic is said to be able to obtain information about an individual through paranormal means by making physical contact with an object that belongs to them. Psychometry has, in recent years, been superseded by "token-object reading".

Psychokinesis: The mental control of physical objects, including effects such as influencing the fall of dice by concentration.

Remote Viewing: Refers to the attempt to gather information about a distant or unseen target using paranormal means or extra-sensory perception. Typically, a remote viewer is expected to give information about an object that is hidden from physical view and separated at some distance.

Retrocognition: The knowledge of past events in the absence of information about those events. It is the exact opposite of precognition.

Second Sight: A form of extra-sensory perception in which a person perceives information, in the form of vision, about future events before they happen.

Stripper Deck: A deck that allows the performer to easily control the location of a card or group of cards within the pack. Even after being shuffled into the deck, the performer can cut to a selected card; or after being lost in different parts of the deck, the performer can control multiple cards to the bottom or top of the deck with a few simple shuffles. This deck has special benefits in performing mentalism effects involving the use of cards.

Telepathy: The ability to transfer thoughts or feelings from the mind of one individual to that of another (or between groups of people), without using the ordinary five senses. Telepathy differs from clairvoyance in that the information comes from the mind of another person.

Thumb tip: A magician's prop used for vanishing, producing, or switching small objects.

* For additional information:

(1) http://www.thefreedictionary.com

(2) http://en.wikipedia.org

(3) http://www.skepdic.com/hotreading.html

(4) http://en.wiktionary.org

REFERENCES AND FURTHER STUDY

Chapter One

13 Steps to Mentalism, by Corinda, 1968.

How to Handle Hecklers: The complete guide to dealing with every performer's worst nightmare! by Keith Fields, 120 pages, soft back (www.keithfields.co.uk)

Magic and Showmanship: A handbook for conjurers, by Henning Nelms, pg. 59-62, 2000.

Chapter Two

Cut Force or X Force: *Self-Working Mental Magic*, by Karl Fulves

pg. 47-48, 1979. Many other methods are available to force a card and can be found in books on card magic.

Dual Vision: This effect is credited to J.G. Thompson, Jr., and further refined by Karl Fulves, of an effect called Future Vision in *Self-Working Mental Magic*, pg. 26-28. In this presentation, all sleight of hand requirements have been removed and emphasis placed on presentation.

Tossed Out Deck: (1) *The Bold and Subtle Miracles of Dr. Faust,* by David Hoy. pg. 25-29. 1975. (2) *Sphinx*, Vol 7, December, 1908. (3) *VideoMind, Phase Two - Close up Mentalism,* by Max Maven, Tossed - Out Tech, 1997.

Card Calling: (1) "Extra Sensational Perception Deck", by George Sands, is available at http://alansands.com. (2) *No Camera Tricks*, by Richard Osterlind, 20 card test. 2007. (3) *Mental Miracles*, by Bob Cassidy, card memory, 1997.

Chapter Three

202 Methods of Forcing, Theodore Annemann (see: www.trickshop. com)

http://www.mathsisfun.com/1089.html

Impromptu Mathematical Precognition (IMP Experiment): This is an adaptation of the effect "Alice in Numberland" found in Robert Mandelberg's *Easy Mind-Reading Tricks*, pg. 25-28, 2005.

Number Please, Richard Busch, 2002.

Chapter Four

Bank Note Revelation: This routine is a standard of mentalism and has been described by many performers. The basis for the "bill switch" is described in *Practical Mental Magic*, by Theodore Annemann, pg. 13-15, 2008. The routine describes a "billet switch" in which a folded dollar bill can be used in place of the billet.

Chapter Five

One Ahead System: (1) *13 Steps to Mentalism*, by Corinda, pg.136, 190-191, 1968. (2) *Practical Mental Magic,* by Theodore Annemann, pg.133-137, 2008.

Chapter Six

Drawing Duplication: **(1)** *Mind Mysteries: Volume Seven,* by Richard Osterlind, design duplication system, 2005. **(2)** *VideoMind, Phase One-Parlor Mentalism*, by Max Maven, The mind's eye deck, 1997.

Chapter Seven

Book Test: (1) *13 Steps to Mentalism,* by Corinda, pg. 208 (2) *The Tarbell Course in Magic (Volume 4),* by Harlan Tarbell, pg.192-196, 1992.

(3) *VideoMind, Phase One- Parlor Mentalism*, by Max Maven, Autome, 1997.

Magician's Choice / Equivoque: *Verbal Control,* by Phil Goldstein, 2003.

INDEX

ABOUT THE AUTHOR

Dr. James E. Jones has been involved with magic and performance mentalism for over 45 years. His professional career has been in health and healthcare education at the university level. He has held faculty and administrative academic appointments at four universities in the United States. He is a member of the International Brotherhood of Magicians and the Society of American Magicians. Additionally, he is a Certified Hypnotist and member of the National Guild of Hypnotists.